Growing Readers

SAFE AND SOUND

Safety First

Angela Royston

Heinemann Library
Des Plaines, Illinois

Customer Service 1-888-454-2279

Text designed by Celia Floyd
Printed and bound in Hong Kong,China

04 03 02 01 00
10 9 8 7 6 5 4 3 2 1

Library of Congress Cataloging-in-Publication Data
Royston, Angela.
      Safety first / Angela Royston.
          p. cm. – (Safe and sound)
      Includes bibliographical references.
      Summary: Explores basic safety rules for daily living, including tips for crossing the street, riding a bicycle, dressing appropriately for the weather, swimming, and getting help in an emergency.
      ISBN 1-57572-984-9
      1. Child rearing—United States Juvenile literature. 2. Safety education—United States Juvenile literature. 3. Children's accidents—United States—Prevention Juvenile literature.
      4. Children—United States—Conduct of life Juvenile literature.
      [1. Safety.} I. Title. II. Series: Royston, Angela. Safe and sound.
      HQ770.7.R69 1999
      613.6—dc21   99-14559
                                                                            CIP

Acknowledgments
The Publishers would like to thank the following for permission to reproduce photographs: Allsport/S. Bruty, p. 10; Andrew Brilliant, p. 19; Bubbles/A. Compton, p. 14; A. Hampton, p. 15; L. Thurston, p. 9; J. Woodcock, p. 21; J. Allan Cash Ltd., pp. 5, 17, 24, 25; Trevor Clifford, pp. 4, 10, 18, 22, 23, 26, 28, 29; Collections/J. Greene, p. 16; PowerStock, p. 20; Science Photo Library/B. Orchidee, p. 7; Stockfile, p. 12; S. Behr, p. 13; Tony Stone Images/R. Daemmrich, p. 27; D. Woodfall, p. 6; Telegraph Color Library/P. von Stroheim, p. 8.

Cover photo: Allsport/S. Bruty

Every effort has been made to contact copyright holders of any material reproduced in this book. Any omissions will be rectified in subsequent printings if notice is given to the Publisher.

The Publishers would like to thank Julie Johnson, PSHE consultant and trainer, for her comments in the preparation of this book.

Some words in this book are in bold, **like this.** You can find out what they mean by looking in the glossary.

Contents

Follow the Rules

When you travel by car, always fasten the seat belt. This is such an important rule that in many states it is a **law**.

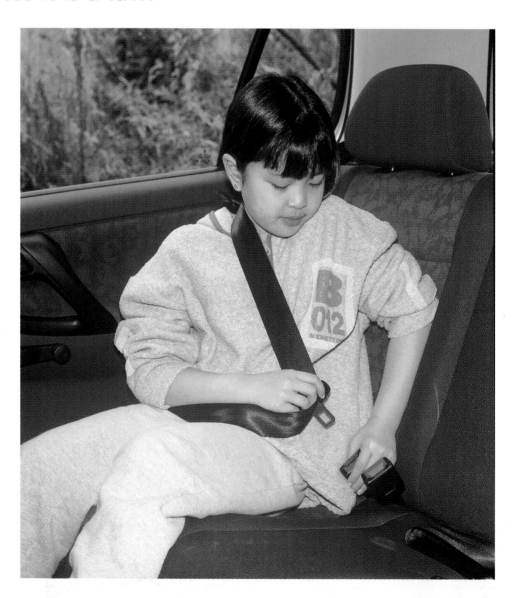

Other rules and signs help to protect you at home, at school, and outdoors. Follow the rules so you can play safely and have fun.

BEWARE OF THE BULL

Poisons and Medicines

This sign means **poison**. Poisons can hurt your body. Never touch or swallow them. Bathroom and kitchen cleaners often are poison.

6

Medicines can make you better, but the wrong medicines can make you sick. It is very dangerous to swallow any medicines that are not meant for you.

Crossing the Street

When you have to cross the street, use a **crosswalk,** or wait until the walk lights show green for **pedestrians.**

If the street does not have a crosswalk, cross with a grown-up. Wait until there is no **traffic**. Look left, right, and left again before you cross.

Dressed for Action

These clothes are good for playing in. Jeans protect your skin and strong shoes protect your feet. **Avoid** clothes with strings that tie at the neck—they may **choke** you.

Do you like skating? Always wear a helmet. Wear pads on your knees, elbows, and wrists. That way you won't hurt yourself so much if you fall.

Safe Cycling

Make sure you wear safe clothes when you ride your bike. Close-fitting long pants or shorts are best, because they won't catch in the wheels.

Always remember to wear a bicycle helmet. This is the right way to put it on. The helmet should fit tightly on top of your head. It should not tip to the front or back of your head.

Covering Up

The sun's rays can hurt your eyes and skin. Wear sunglasses. Use **sunblock** to protect your skin.

Be careful how much time you spend in the sun. The sun's rays are strongest from 10 A.M. to 4 P.M. each day. Wear a T-shirt and sunhat to protect your skin and eyes.

Safe Swimming

Arm floats keep you safe when you learn to swim. You should read and follow the rules of the swimming pool, too.

Some beaches have a **lifeguard** who watches to make sure everyone is safe. Flags sometimes show where it is safe to swim. Never swim where there is no lifeguard or another grown-up to watch you.

Water Safety

If something falls in the water, stay on the side and use a stick to get it out. The water may be deep! In winter, never walk out on the ice.

Wear a **life jacket** if you go in a boat or canoe, even if you can swim. The life jacket will keep you **afloat** if you fall in the water.

19

Fire Safety

It's easy to blow out the candles on a birthday cake, but matches can start fires that cannot be blown out. Never play with matches.

Many families have a cookout in warm weather. It is fun to watch the food cooking, but keep away from the grill and the hot, burning coals.

Safe at Home

Be careful when you take food out of a toaster.
Never use anything metal to pick up the food.
Never poke anything into machines or plugs.
Electricity can give you a
dangerous **electric shock**.

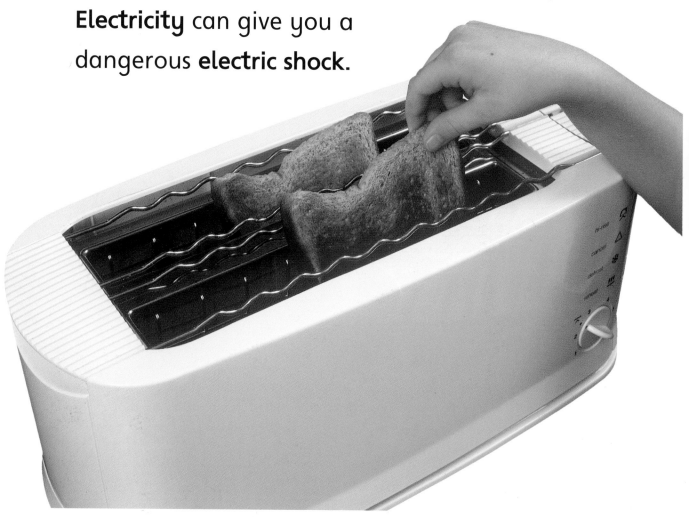

Irons, toasters, and stoves can get very hot. They stay hot after they have been turned off, so keep away until they have cooled down.

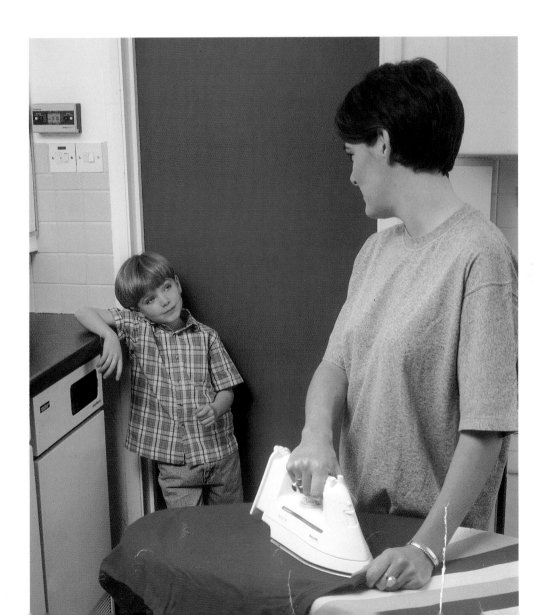

Playing Safely

A building **site** is not a safe place to play. When you want to run and climb, go to a park or a playground.

Keep away from railroad tracks. Trains travel very fast and they cannot stop quickly. There may also be dangerous **power lines** by train tracks.

On Your Own

In a store, do not wander off on your own. If you do get lost, tell a **salesperson.** He or she will help you find the adult you are with.

Some people are dangerous. If someone you don't know asks you to go with them, say no. Shout very loudly if you need help.

Getting Help

The police, ambulance service, and firefighters are always ready to help in an emergency. To call them, dial 911 and tell them where you are.

The 911 operator will ask you some questions. Listen carefully. Stay on the phone until the operator says to go.

Don't let a grown-up or another child hurt you or make you do things you think are wrong. Tell an adult you trust, such as a parent or teacher.

Glossary

afloat   staying on the surface of something, such as water

avoid   to try not to do something

choke   to keep you from breathing

crosswalk   part of a street that has been marked off for people to use when crossing

electricity   power that makes some machines work

electric shock   kind of injury caused by electric current passing through the body

law   rule that tells people what they should and should not do

lifeguard   person at a beach or swimming pool who watches out for people who might need help

life jacket   special vest made of cork or other light material that will float

medicine   something that is taken by mouth or used on the body to take away pain or treat a disease

pedestrian   someone who is walking

poison   substance that makes you sick or can kill you if you swallow it or breathe it in

power line   heavy wires and towers that bring electricity to a place

salesperson   someone who works in a store

site   piece of land where something will be built

sunblock   cream or lotion that helps protect skin from the sun's rays

traffic   cars and trucks traveling along the road

Index

More Books to Read

Loewen, Nancy. *Bicycle Safety*. Chanhassen, Minn.: Child's World, 1996.

—. *Emergencies.* Chanhassen, Minn.: Child's World, 1996.

Mattern, Joanne. *Safety at Home*. Minneapolis: ABDO Publishing Company, 1999.